LEECHES

by Katie Marsico

Children's Press®

An Imprint of Scholastic Inc.

Content Consultant
Dr. Stephen S. Ditchkoff
Professor of Wildlife Sciences
Auburn University
Auburn, Alabama

Photographs ©: cover: Geoff Tompkinson/Science Source; 1: Arco Images GmbH/Alamy Images; 2 background, 3 background: Xiaowen Sun/Dreamstime; 2, 3: Ted Kinsman/Science Source; 4, 5 background: Tim Laman/National Geographic Creative; 5 top inset: David J Slate/Getty Images; 5 bottom inset: RIA Novosti/The Image Works; 6, 7: Animals Animals/Superstock, Inc.; 8: Arco Images GmbH/Alamy Images; 10, 11: Ted Kinsman/Science Source; 12, 13: Minden Pictures/Superstock, Inc.; 14, 15: Sydeen/Dreamstime; 16, 17: David J Slate/Getty Images; 18, 19: Eye of Science/Science Source; 20, 21: blickwinkel/Alamy Images; 22, 23: Martin Dohrn/Getty Images; 24, 25: Tim Laman/National Geographic Creative; 26, 27: Biosphoto/Superstock, Inc.; 28, 29: Auscape/UIG/age fotostock; 31: The Natural History Museum/Alamy Images; 32: Prisma/Superstock, Inc.; 35: Louise Murray/Science Source; 36, 37: Steve Hopkins/Ardea/Animals Animals; 39: Scientifica/Visuals Unlimited; 40, 41: RIA Novosti/The Image Works; 44 background, 45 background: Xiaowen Sun/Dreamstime; 46: Arco Images GmbH/Alamy Image.

Library of Congress Cataloging-in-Publication Data
Marsico, Katie, 1980– author.
  Leeches / by Katie Marsico.
    pages cm. – (Nature's children)
  Summary: "This book details the life and habits of leeches"– Provided by publisher.
  Includes bibliographical references and index.
  ISBN 978-0-531-21394-0 (library binding : alk. paper) — ISBN 978-0-531-21497-8 (pbk. : alk. paper)
  1. Leeches—Juvenile literature. I. Title. II. Series: Nature's children (New York, N.Y.)
  QL391.A6M27 2016
  592.66—dc23   2014046960

Printed in China 62
SCHOLASTIC, CHILDREN'S PRESS, and associated logos are trademarks and/or registered trademarks of Scholastic Inc.

1 2 3 4 5 6 7 8 9 10 R 25 24 23 22 21 20 19 18 17 16

Leeches

Class	Clitellata
Subclass	Hirudinea
Orders	Rhynchobdellida and Arhynchobdellida
Families and Genera	There are many leech families and genera, but scientists are still working to classify them precisely
Species	Around 700 species
World distribution	Worldwide
Habitats	Freshwater (lakes, ponds, rivers, streams, and swamps), marine (estuaries, oceans, and seas), and terrestrial (typically rain forests and wooded coastal environments)
Distinctive physical characteristics	Average length of 0.8 to 2 inches (2 to 5 centimeters); has either no jaws or up to three sets of jaws; form is flattened, and thins out toward the front end; skin is shades of black, brown, and dark green
Habits	Generally solitary, except during mating season or brooding; often nocturnal; some species can go up to a year between meals; hides in soil or among rocks and plant life; parasitic species spend time attached to host organisms to feed on the organisms' blood
Diet	Parasitic species feed on the blood of fish, frogs, turtles, birds, mammals, and even other leeches; nonparasitic species eat snails, insects, and worms

Contents

CHAPTER 1

Feasting on Frog Blood

Mosquitoes and dragonflies buzz over the still surface of a pond in the northeastern United States. A bullfrog sits near the water's edge quietly searching for **prey**. Yet, as the frog waits to feed, it has already become a food source itself!

Stretched across the frog's back is a leech. At first, this thick, flat worm appears motionless. However, it is busily sucking the bullfrog's blood. Once it is full, the leech relaxes its jaws. Swollen to several times its normal weight, it drops to the muddy shoreline. Meanwhile, the bullfrog leaps away, unaware that the leech was ever there.

Leeches are **annelid** worms with suckers on either end of their body. Many are also bloodsucking parasites. Parasites depend on other organisms to survive but typically offer few benefits in return. This is not always true of leeches, though. Some doctors use these animals to address blood flow issues in human patients!

Leeches are best known for their ability to attach themselves to unsuspecting hosts.

Where Leeches Live

Leeches live in a broad range of **habitats**. They are found all over the world, including in icy Antarctic waters. Scientists believe there are approximately 700 **species** of leeches. Most of these annelids dwell in freshwater environments. A few examples are lakes, ponds, swamps, streams, and rivers. Other leeches exist in marine areas such as **estuaries**, seas, and oceans. Finally, certain species live in terrestrial, or land-based, habitats. These leeches tend to prefer warm, moist surroundings such as rain forests and wooded coastal environments.

Leeches frequently hide in soil or among rocks and plant life. In dry, cool weather, some species bury themselves in mud until conditions become wetter and warmer. Parasitic leeches also spend some of their time attached to hosts. Hosts are the animals that parasites feed on in order to survive.

Different leech species live in a wide variety of environments.

An Overview of Appearance

Most leeches are various shades of brown, black, and dark green. They typically measure 0.8 to 2 inches (2 to 5 centimeters) long. The largest species—the giant Amazon leech—sometimes grows up to 18 inches (46 cm) long. That's roughly the distance between a person's elbow and fingertips.

A leech's bilaterally symmetrical form thins out toward its front end. Organisms with bilateral symmetry have identical characteristics on both their left and right sides. Meanwhile, a leech's front and rear ends each feature a sucker. The sucker surrounding the mouth is usually the smaller of the two. In addition, leeches—like other annelids—are **invertebrates** and have a **segmented** body.

Some leeches have up to three jaws, while others have no jaws at all. They also have **eyespots** that are sensitive to changes in light. Just behind a leech's head is a raised band of tissue called a clitellum. The clitellum contains fluid used during **reproduction**.

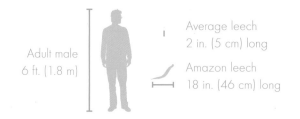

Adult male
6 ft. (1.8 m)

Average leech
2 in. (5 cm) long

Amazon leech
18 in. (46 cm) long

Some leeches are extremely small.

11

CHAPTER 2

Incredible Adaptations

Leeches may seem like simple creatures. However, they have several amazing features that have helped them survive for hundreds of millions of years.

In the wild, leeches face many different kinds of predators. Aquatic species are hunted by fish, snakes, turtles, and birds such as ducks. Meanwhile, leeches found on land are eaten by animals ranging from monkeys to lizards. Mites and snails have also been known to devour leech eggs.

Strangely, leeches often feed on the same kinds of creatures that hunt them. Some common hosts for parasitic leeches are fish, frogs, turtles, birds, and mammals—including people! It is also not unusual for leeches to suck each other's blood. Certain types of leeches don't feed on blood at all. These nonparasitic species swallow their prey whole. They mainly eat snails, insects, and worms.

Leeches make tasty snacks for snipes and many other types of birds.

Senses Supporting Survival

Leeches don't have ears, so they can't rely on hearing to avoid predators and find food. Instead, they depend on other senses to gather information about the world around them. A leech's vision isn't powerful enough to see images the way humans and many other animals do. However, its eyespots allow it to observe changes in light and possibly motion. This is especially useful to the many leeches that are nocturnal. Being sensitive to how shadows develop and shift makes it easier for leeches to search for food in the dark. This also makes it easier for nocturnal leeches to avoid predators that typically hunt during the night.

Sensilla are another important feature for a leech. These basic organs are found within a leech's soft, moist skin. They detect vibrations that signal nearby movement. Leeches also sense changes in their environment through taste and smell. For example, the odor and flavor of water alert aquatic leeches to the location of potential predators and hosts.

Eyespots are tiny, dark spots located at the end of a leech's head.

Meaningful Motion

Scientists have observed a wide range of movement in leeches. When they sense food or danger, leeches will often stretch out to their full length. They then remain completely still. This increases the sensitivity of their sensilla to outside vibrations and chemical changes.

After detecting a nearby food source, leeches approach it by squeezing and stretching their powerful, flexible muscles. In the water, they make wavelike movements that propel them forward. On land, their motion closely resembles that of inchworms. Leeches use their front sucker to attach to whatever animal or object they are trying to reach.

When fleeing from a predator, some leeches squeeze and stretch to swim or crawl away. Other species respond to attacks by curling up in a ball and dropping to the ground. Afterward, they relax their muscles, go limp, and stay motionless. Scientists suspect this is their attempt at "playing dead." Once predators no longer notice movement, they are more likely to lose interest and abandon the chase.

A leech extends its body forward as it waits for a host to pass by.

Feeding Features

Leeches have several features to help them feed. Species such as the European medicinal leech have three muscular jaws lined with tiny teeth called denticles. After locating a tender area in a host's flesh, these leeches move their denticles back and forth over it. The sawing motion of their jaws forms a Y-shaped cut. Species that have only two jaws—such as the Australian land leech—eat in a similar manner. However, they leave a V-shaped bite mark.

Jawless leeches lack teeth altogether. They use a long, tube-shaped mouthpart called a proboscis to create puncture wounds in prey. When jawless leeches aren't feeding, they pull their proboscis back into a sheath, or covering, on their head.

Nonparasitic leeches such as the Kinabalu giant red leech have neither teeth nor a proboscis. They don't need these features because they don't suck blood. Instead, they use their large jaws to swallow worms and young insects whole.

This close-up of a leech's mouth shows its rows of sharp denticles.

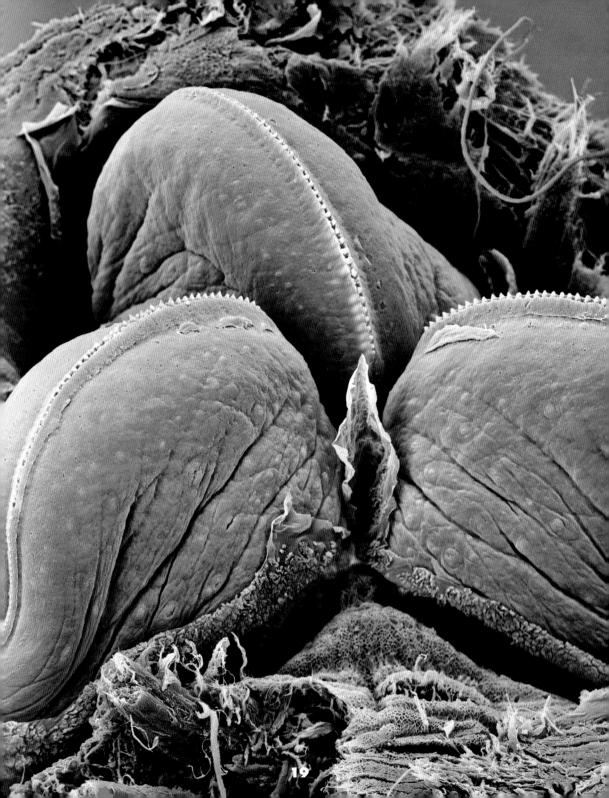

Substances in the Saliva

Piercing the flesh of a host is only half the challenge for parasitic leeches. They also need to be able to feed without interruption. If leeches created discomfort while biting or eating, host organisms would try to attack or remove them. This means leeches must keep hosts unaware of their presence.

Scientists think parasitic leeches have adapted to this challenge by producing a chemical that acts like an **anesthetic**. When they puncture a host's flesh, the area is temporarily numbed. As a result, hosts don't feel leeches sucking their blood.

The **saliva** of parasitic leeches contains other important chemicals as well. Some of these substances widen the host's blood vessels. This causes blood to flow more freely. In addition, leeches release a chemical called hirudin. Hirudin prevents blood **cells** from clotting, or sticking together. Without hirudin, blood would thicken once inside a leech's digestive system. This would lead to harmful blockages within the parasite's body.

A leech's saliva has anesthetic qualities that prevent a host from noticing its presence.

A Look at Leech Digestion

Leeches are ferocious feeders. Some have been known to consume up to 10 times their own body weight in just 31 minutes. When leeches eat, they bloat, or swell, like a balloon. Normally, bloating makes it hard for most animals to move. However, leeches don't face this problem, thanks to a naturally produced chemical called serotonin. Serotonin helps their strained muscles continue stretching. As a result, leeches are able to stay in motion even when bloated.

After parasitic leeches feed, they typically search for a hiding place under rocks or plants. On reaching such a destination, some can rest for an entire year before eating again! This is because parasitic leeches have a slow digestive system. It often takes them several months to fully digest a single meal. A parasitic leech is also able to go long periods between feedings because its gut features multiple pouches. These pouches are capable of storing large amounts of blood.

Leeches can grow very large when they are full of blood.

23

CHAPTER 3

A Leech's Life Cycle

Life spans vary for different leech species. Some of these annelids live just a few months. Scientists believe others might survive up to 20 years.

Leeches tend to be solitary animals. They spend much of their life alone, rather than in groups. One exception to this rule is **mating** season, which usually occurs throughout spring and summer. Leeches rely on their sense of touch and the natural chemicals they produce to locate mates.

During their life cycle, leeches develop both male and female reproductive organs. However, this doesn't mean they are capable of reproducing on their own. One of the main reasons is because they don't always have both sets of organs at the same time.

The age at which leeches become ready for reproduction is different among the various species. For example, some parasitic species don't reach maturity until they have at least three blood meals.

Two leeches engage in a mating dance atop a leaf.

The Contents of Cocoons

In general, leeches only reproduce once or twice throughout their life cycle. During mating season, their clitellum becomes larger and more visible. This is because it releases thick fluid that is used to form cocoons. Leeches often produce multiple cocoons at once. After a leech mates, the cocoons house its eggs until they hatch.

Some species carry these egg sacs internally or along their underside. Others attach their cocoons to soil, rocks, plants, or even the bodies of nearby host organisms. In many cases, parents abandon their detached cocoons. However, this is not true of all leeches. For example, some jawless species actively care for their unborn young. Parents use their bodies to shield the cocoons from predators and other dangers. It usually takes about two to six weeks for the eggs to hatch.

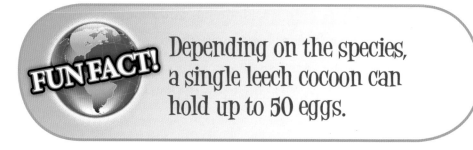

FUN FACT! Depending on the species, a single leech cocoon can hold up to 50 eggs.

Leech cocoons are made of soft, spongy material that protects the eggs inside.

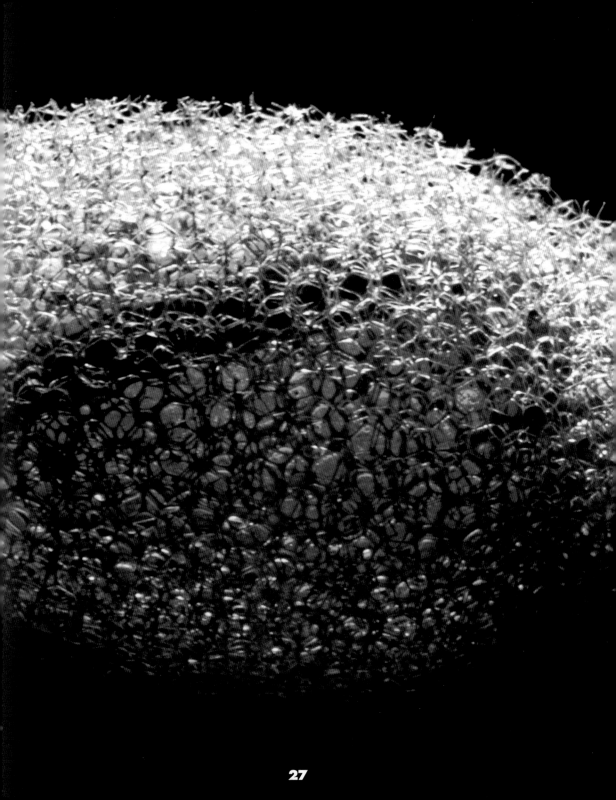

Babies and Brooding

When baby leeches emerge from their cocoon, they look like miniature versions of their parents. Many are immediately independent as well. They quickly seek out host organisms or prey and begin feeding.

Some species receive further care from their parents. For example, newly hatched jawless leeches often remain with adults for an additional three to four weeks. This is commonly referred to as a brooding period.

During the brooding period, leech parents carry their young on their underside. This provides the small, helpless babies with extra protection from predators. In addition, scientists have noted that brooding sometimes involves parents directly feeding juveniles. A leech parent uses its front sucker to grasp snails and offer them to the babies. Once brooding ends, juvenile leeches detach from their parents. Afterward, they travel on their own and don't require any assistance finding food.

A leech carries its young as it swims through the water.

CHAPTER 4

From Past to Present

It is likely that leeches existed even before dinosaurs. The earliest species probably **evolved** from freshwater worms about 540 million years ago. That's about 310 million years before dinosaurs first appeared.

Scientists believe the first leeches were parasites that used a proboscis to suck blood from their hosts. Later, some species developed jaws and teeth. For others, the proboscis became smaller and sometimes disappeared altogether. This made it easier for certain types of leeches to swallow prey whole.

Unfortunately, few **fossils** exist to provide people with additional information about prehistoric annelids. Since leeches are soft-bodied animals, they don't often leave behind hardened remains when they die. However, scientists have discovered different forms of fossilized evidence that offer clues about these animals' evolution. They have even found fossils of leech cocoons that date back hundreds of millions of years!

Fossils of ancient worms have helped scientists understand how leeches have changed throughout time.

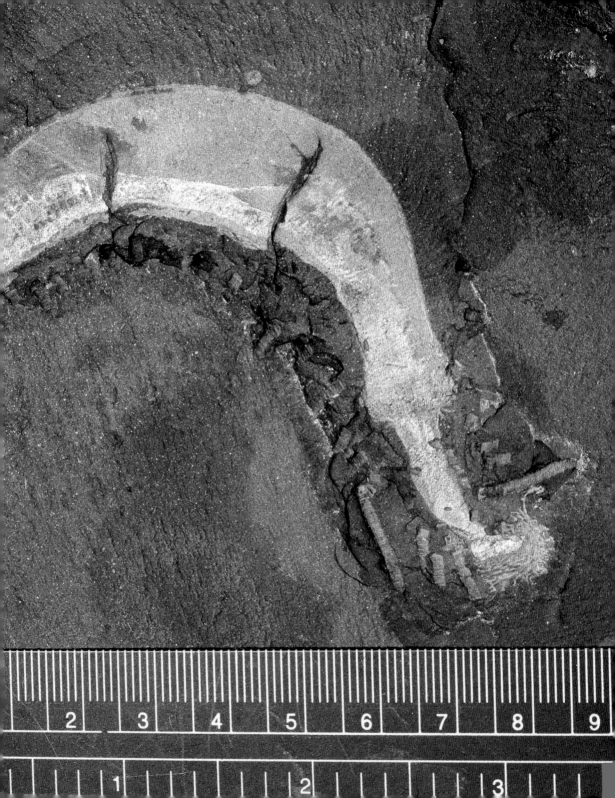

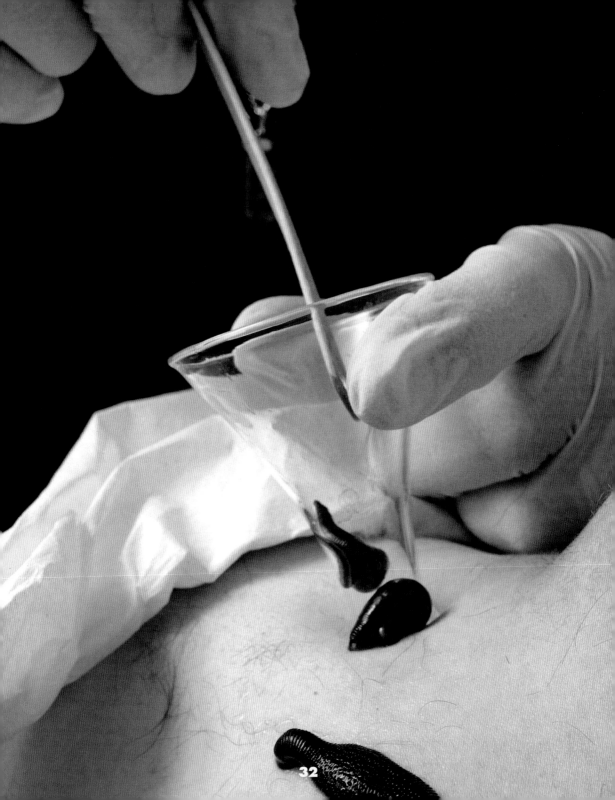

32

Unique Medical Uses

The history of leeches has been shaped by far more than how they evolved. People have used these annelids to practice medicine for thousands of years. Since ancient times, parasitic leeches have played an important role in bloodletting. Bloodletting is a surgical procedure in which a patient's blood is purposely removed to either cure or prevent illness.

For many centuries, doctors involved leeches in bloodletting to treat conditions ranging from poor eyesight to mental health problems. As a result, people set up leech farms to raise and sell the parasites for medical purposes. By the late 1800s, however, leech therapy had grown less common. Doctors began relying more heavily on other medications.

Leeches have recently regained popularity with some medical experts. Some scientists point out that the parasites' saliva improves a person's circulation by preventing clotting and increasing blood flow. Scientists also believe leeches can help doctors treat blood disorders and reattach lost fingers.

Doctors use special equipment to apply medicinal leeches during treatment.

Leech Classification

Not all scientists agree on the best way to chart a family tree for leeches. Some have different opinions about grouping these annelids according to similar characteristics and behaviors. When discussing leeches, however, people are usually referring to "true leeches." A true leech has a sucker on either end of its body.

At present, scientists have identified two **orders** of true leeches. The first—Rhynchobdellida—is made up of jawless leeches that have a proboscis. The second order is Arhynchobdellida, or leeches that lack a proboscis.

People are often most familiar with the European medicinal leech, which is part of the order Arhynchobdellida. As its name indicates, this species is frequently involved in medical procedures. European medicinal leeches are found in freshwater environments throughout Europe. When fully grown, they measure about 8 inches (20 cm) long and have a thin red stripe on their upper side. Though they aren't **endangered**, they're less common than they were before people began harvesting them for medical use.

The European medicinal leech is larger than many other leech species.

Close Annelid Cousins

It's not unusual for people to compare leeches to their close relatives, earthworms. Both animals are segmented invertebrates that have both male and female reproductive organs. Like leeches, earthworms also produce cocoons that hold their eggs until they hatch.

Despite these similarities, there are several big differences between earthworms and leeches. One is that earthworms aren't parasites. Instead, they feed on the nutrients found in soil. In addition, earthworms live mainly in terrestrial habitats. Unlike leeches, they never live in water.

Earthworms tend to be longer and thinner than their annelid cousins. They generally have lighter coloring as well. Finally, earthworms have setae, which leeches lack. Setae are stiff bristles found along the bodies of many invertebrates. These hairs help earthworms attach to and move across various surfaces.

FUN FACT! More than a million earthworms can occupy a single acre of land at the same time.

An earthworm's body is divided into multiple visible segments.

CHAPTER 5

Parasites and People

Leeches and humans share a long, complicated relationship. Regardless of their role in medicine, these annelids are often perceived as pests. This is because some leeches feed by attaching themselves to unsuspecting human hosts who wade into their freshwater habitats. Sometimes the incisions these parasites create in a host's flesh become infected. They have also been known to trigger allergic reactions.

Further problems can occur if people attempt to remove leeches from their skin the wrong way. Simply pulling on leeches while they're still eating can cause wounds to deepen. Burning a leech or putting salt on it aren't necessarily safe techniques either. Such removal methods frequently make leeches regurgitate, or throw up. Since they have bacteria in their gut, regurgitating into an open wound creates potential health problems for hosts. The spread of bacteria increases the risk that a host will get sick.

Leech bites leave behind a distinctive Y-shaped or V-shaped mark.

More Helpful Than Harmful

Scientists are eager to educate both medical professionals and the general public about leeches. They hope to improve people's understanding of these incredible annelids. Ideally, this will prove that leeches can be more helpful than harmful.

Part of their research is focused on the many medical possibilities linked to leech therapy. Just as importantly, however, people are trying to figure out how to peacefully coexist alongside parasitic species. Sometimes this can be as basic as knowing how to safely remove leeches. First, it is usually best to ask an adult for help. Then, experts recommend using a fingernail to gently nudge the leech's front end, which is the thinner end. Eventually, this technique should succeed in pushing the parasite away from any open wounds.

Ultimately, new research and knowledge are helping people realize that leeches are far more than bloodsuckers. What seem like simple—and occasionally pesky—worms are actually rather remarkable animals. Interesting and medically important, leeches are an astounding part of the natural world.

There is still a lot people can learn by studying leeches.

Words to Know

anesthetic (an-is-THET-ik) — a substance capable of preventing or lessening pain

annelid (AN-uh-lid) — a segmented worm

aquatic (uh-KWAT-ik) — living or growing in water

bacteria (bak-TEER-ee-uh) — microscopic, single-celled living things that exist everywhere and can be either useful or harmful

cells (SELZ) — the smallest units that make up living things

circulation (sir-kyeh-LAY-shuhn) — the movement of blood through the body

endangered (en-DAYN-jurd) — at risk of becoming extinct, usually because of human activity

estuaries (ES-choo-er-eez) — the wide parts of rivers that join the ocean

evolved (i-VAHLVD) — changed slowly and naturally over time

eyespots (EYE-spahtz) — simple visual organs that often appear as coloring on the skin

fossils (FOSS-uhlz) — bones, shells, or other traces of animals or plants from millions of years ago, preserved as rock

habitats (HAB-uh-tats) — the places where an animal or a plant is usually found invertebrates (in-VUR-tuh-brits) — animals without backbones

mating (MAYT-ing) — joining together to produce babies

nocturnal (nahk-TUR-nuhl) — active mainly at night

orders (OR-durz) — groups of related plants or animals that are bigger than families but smaller than classes

predators (PREH-duh-turz) — animals that live by hunting other animals for food

prey (PRAY) — animals that are hunted by other animals for food

reproduction (ree-pruh-DUHK-shuhn) — the act of producing offspring or individuals of the same kind

saliva (suh-LYE-vuh) — the watery fluid in a mouth that keeps it moist and helps to soften food, enabling it to be swallowed

segmented (SEG-men-tid) — divided into sections

species (SPEE-sheez) — one of the groups into which animals and plants of the same genus are divided

Habitat Map

Leech Range on Land
Note: *Leeches are also found throughout the world's oceans.*

NORTH AMERICA

SOUTH AMERICA

PACIFIC OCEAN

ATLANTIC OCEAN

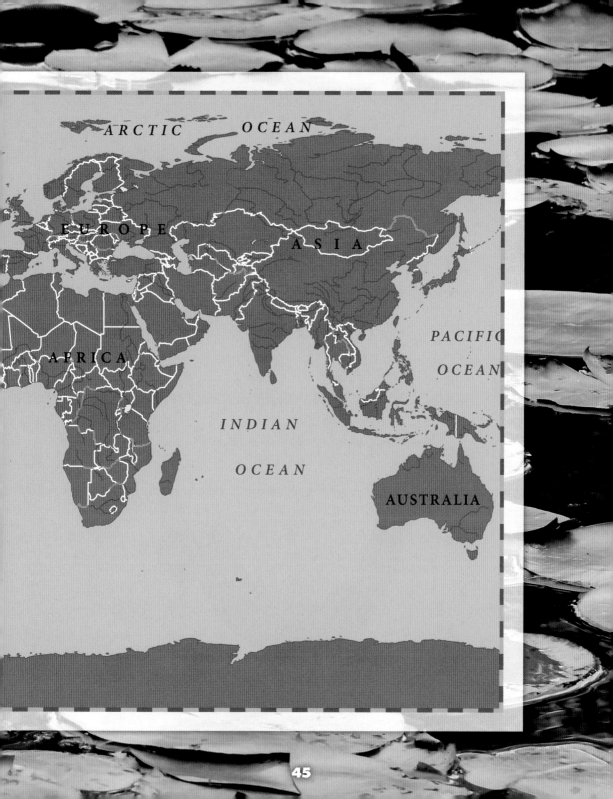

ARCTIC OCEAN

EUROPE

ASIA

AFRICA

PACIFIC OCEAN

INDIAN OCEAN

AUSTRALIA

Find Out More

Books

Coleman, Miriam. *Leeches Eat Blood!* New York: PowerKids Press, 2014.

Kopp, Megan. *Parasites.* New York: AV2 by Weigl, 2012.

Parker, Steve. *Nematodes, Leeches & Other Worms.* Minneapolis: Compass Point Books, 2006.

Visit this Scholastic Web site for more information on leeches:
www.factsfornow.scholastic.com
Enter the keyword **Leeches**

Index

Page numbers in *italics* indicate a photograph or map.

About the Author

Katie Marsico is the author of nearly 200 children's books. After writing *Leeches*, she gained an entirely new appreciation for how amazing these annelids truly are. In spite of that, Ms. Marsico hopes that she never gains any firsthand experience when it comes to leech therapy.